# WILT!

## THE SPORTS CAREER OF WILTON CHAMBERLAIN

BY:

# JAMES & LYNN HAHN

EDITED BY:

# DR. HOWARD SCHROEDER

Professor in Reading and Language Arts
Dept. of Elementary Education
Mankato State University

## CRESTWOOD HOUSE

Mankato, Minnesota

# CIP

**LIBRARY OF CONGRESS CATALOGING IN PUBLICATION DATA**

Hahn, James.
  Wilt! The sports career of Wilton Chamberlain.

  (Sports legends)
  SUMMARY: Presents a biography of the 7-foot basketball player who set many NBA scoring records during his long career.
    1. Chamberlain, Wilton Norman, 1936-      — Juvenile literature. 2. Basketball players — United States — Biography — Juvenile literature. 3. National Basketball Association — Juvenile literature. [1. Chamberlain, Wilton Norman, 1936-    . 2. Basketball players. 3. Afro-Americans — Biography] I. Hahn, Lynn, joint author. II. Schroeder, Howard. III. Title. IV. Series.
GV884.C5H33          796.32'3'0924      [B]   [92]          80-28746
ISBN 0-89686-124-4 (lib. bdg.)
ISBN 0-89686-139-2 (pbk.)

| INTERNATIONAL STANDARD BOOK NUMBERS: | LIBRARY OF CONGRESS CATALOG CARD NUMBER: |
|---|---|
| 0-89686-124-4 Library Bound<br>0-89686-139-2 Paperback | 80-28746 |

# PHOTO CREDITS:

Cover: Focus on Sports, Inc.

Wide World Photos: 3, 15, 31, 39
UPI: 5, 8, 13, 16, 19, 20, 22, 24-25, 26, 28, 32, 35, 38, 40-41, 43, 45
FPG/Lawrence Agron: 36, 46

CRESTWOOD HOUSE

**Crestwood House, Inc., Box 3427, Hwy. 66 So., Mankato, MN 56001**

# WILT!

# CHAPTER 1

Who scored one hundred points in a National Basketball Association (NBA) game? Who averaged fifty points per game in a pro season and scored more points than anyone in the NBA? Who was the top rebounder in the NBA and the only center to lead the NBA in assists?

Who broke more NBA records than all other players combined and held sixty-four NBA records at one time? Who broke eighteen NBA records at age thirty-seven?

There is only one person who could have done all that, Wilton Norman Chamberlain.

Here's one more surprising fact about Wilt. He never fouled out of an NBA game! "I'm proud of that record," Wilt said. "I get paid to help my team. I can't help them if I'm on the bench or in the shower."

Teamwork meant a lot to Wilt. In 1967 he helped the Philadelphia 76ers win the NBA title. Later, in 1972, Wilt and the Los Angeles Lakers won the crown.

A roller coaster ride with lots of ups, downs, twists, and turns is one way to describe Wilt's life. Living was seldom easy for this complex, outspoken

4

sports legend.

Wilt was born on August 21, 1936. The Chamberlain family did not live in a wealthy neighborhood. Their home was on the west side of Philadelphia. It had a living room, dining room, and basement. A fenced-in roof on top of the garage gave the children a place to play. The house had four bedrooms. "So," Wilt said, "we doubled up on sleeping. We even slept four in a bed when the girls were younger."

Nine children sat around the Chamberlain din-

**Wilt led the Los Angeles Lakers to the 1972 NBA crown.**

ner table. Wilt was in the middle. Wilt's father worked as a welder in a shipyard. Later, he worked as a handyman for a department store. Then he had a job as a janitor for a publishing firm. "I doubt that he ever took home more than $62 a week," Wilt stated. Wilt's mother worked as a maid.

Wilt never missed a meal. "I never had to make do with a skimpy portion," he said. For supper, the family often ate pork chops or pot roast. Their meals never lacked important vitamins and minerals. Breakfasts on Sundays were special for the Chamberlain family. They had orange juice, milk, coffee, eggs, toast, sausage, bacon, and fish.

Although his parents didn't have much money, Wilt had everything important. "I never went to school without shoes or clean clothes," Wilt said. He wore his older brother's hand-me-downs. "When you come from a family of nine, there's a lot to hand down."

Love guided the Chamberlains through hard times. Wilt's parents were devoted to each other and their children. "I think their record," Wilt smiled, "if you can call it that, speaks for itself." His parents had been married for forty-six years when his father died in 1968. "All nine of their children made something of themselves," Wilt said. "None of us wound up hurt, on welfare, or in jail."

One thing did bother Wilt when he was young. There was a trolley bus barn one block from his home. Every morning at 5:30 the trolley buses roared by his bedroom window. "Those buses shook me out of bed in a hurry," he said.

Working together helped the Chamberlain family. They all put their earnings into the family pot. Wilt got his first jobs when he was just five years old. First, he sold newspapers. Then, he washed windows, shoveled snow, and cleaned peoples' basements. Sometimes he pulled his wagon down to the food store. He helped people take their bags of groceries home. The pennies and nickels earned were given to his mother.

At age six, Wilt got up at five o'clock in the morning. He helped the milkman unload wooden crates full of milk bottles. Wilt also picked up empty bottles and took them to the truck.

# CHAPTER

As a young person, Wilt was tall. His height caused him problems when he was only seven years old. By that age, he was already eight or ten inches taller than most children. "I'd go to the movies with my family and friends," he said. "They'd get in for children's prices. I had to pay adult prices, which you didn't have to pay until you were eleven. The

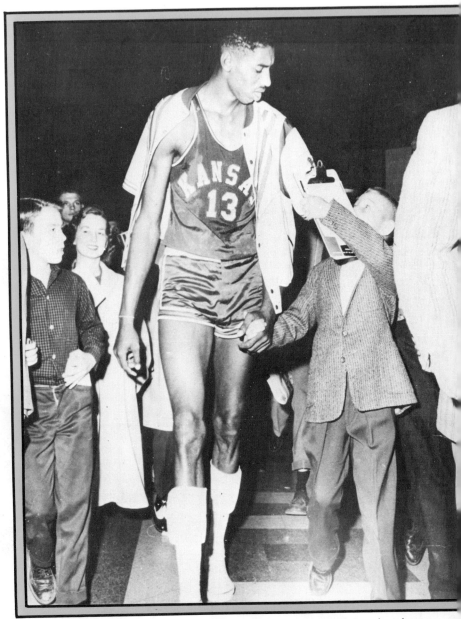

Even though he didn't like it, the name, Wilt the Stilt, stuck with him for obvious reasons. Here Wilt talks to a young fan when he played for the University of Kansas.

woman in the booth thought I had to be older because I was so tall."

At that time, some people called him "Wilt the Stilt." That was one name Wilt didn't like. He felt people were making fun of his long, thin legs. His brothers, sisters, and friends called him "Dip" or "Dippy." They used those names because he was so tall he had to dip under doorways. Later, people called him "Dipper" and "Big Dipper."

Junk interested young Wilt. He saved scraps of iron, tin, brass, and rags, cans, cardboard, and papers. Wilt searched for these types of things everywhere. He even looked in alleys, trash cans, and vacant lots. Wilt collected a lot of junk by going door-to-door and asking for paper and cans. Soon, people started saving these things for him.

On some Saturday mornings, Wilt collected two hundred pounds of junk. He took it to the junkyard and was paid eight or nine cents a pound for it.

Wilt gave his mother half the money. Then he took his sisters to the movies, and bought them popcorn and ice cream.

One day, when he was eight, Wilt went to the basement looking for rags and junk to sell. He picked through many boxes and bags and took the things he thought would get the best prices. Wilt sold the "junk" for two dollars.

A few months later, Wilt's mother was in the

basement putting away winter clothes and taking out summer clothes. Suddenly, she screamed!

Wilt had sold almost all the family's summer clothes! For his punishment, Wilt couldn't go out for two weeks.

Wilt always enjoyed running. "As a young kid," he said, "I ran a lot. I ran to the store, school, friends' houses, back home — everywhere!" All that running helped make Wilt a fast, strong runner.

When Wilt was in fourth grade, coaches chose him to run in the 1946 Penn Relays. Wilt ran very well and won some medals and ribbons.

When the relays were finished, Wilt became very ill and almost died from pneumonia. After slipping in and out of a coma for several months, he finally recovered.

Illness didn't stop Wilt's growth. By age ten, he was six feet tall.

At age eleven, Wilt got another job. After school, he sold melons and tomatoes from his wagon. During the summer, Wilt and his friends painted houses.

For many years Wilt had the bad habit of sucking his thumb. "I sure must have looked weird," Wilt said. "I walked around with my big thumb jammed in my mouth. At that time I was twelve and stood six foot three."

When Wilt was thirteen he went to a summer camp, but didn't like it. "I wound up working seventeen hours a day," he said. "I washed dishes, pots and pans, and only earned thirteen cents an hour."

However, Wilt said all the work he did as a boy helped him later in life. "Jobs taught me the value of a dollar and the value of my own work," he said. "I learned how to bargain and judge people, prices, and services."

Track and field sports still excited Wilt. Shot-putting was his favorite. Every day he spent two or three hours putting the shot. Wilt didn't care if it was raining, snowing, or hailing! "I'd wallow in the mud if I had to," he said. "I'd practice and practice, the year around. That's why I won medals and ribbons."

# CHAPTER 3

Basketball didn't interest Wilt when he was young. "I always thought it was a sissy game," he said. "It didn't seem like a very tough game. It wasn't like running or playing football. I just didn't have any desire to play the game."

In junior high school, other students kept razzing Wilt. "As tall as you are," they laughed, "you should try basketball."

So the students would stop teasing him, Wilt

decided to give basketball a try. That was the first time he played the sport.

Wilt enjoyed basketball very much. He played after school every day until dark. Then he ran home for supper. After supper, he ran back to the basketball courts and played more.

Wilt couldn't get enough basketball. One night he tried to play in his basement and broke the plumbing. It cost $85 to repair.

Soon, basketball was the most important thing in Wilt's life. He spent most of his time at the Haddington Recreation Center. Wilt played in church and school leagues, and in the Police Athletic League.

Wilt's height helped him play the center position well. When he was fourteen years old, he was six feet seven inches tall.

By the time Wilt was in the ninth grade, college and pro scouts were watching him play. Many high schools wanted him to play on their teams. One school even offered Wilt clothes, bus fare, and lunch money if he played for them. Wilt chose to go to Overbrook High, the public school near his home in Philadelphia.

Wilt wasn't a great basketball player just because he was tall. He worked hard building his skills and was willing to give up things. He practiced afternoons, evenings, and weekends. During the summer, he practiced all day long. Wilt worked on

**Wilt was probably the best rebounder that ever played the game. He began to learn the skill in ninth grade.**

dribbling, shooting, passing, rebounding, and free-throws.

Thinking only about basketball was one more key to Wilt's success. "Some guys can think hard for a short time," Wilt said. "But, then their thoughts wander. I've always been able to think about something as long as I've had to. I put my mind to it and shut out everything else."

In his first varsity game, Wilt scored thirty-two points. During the season, he scored thirty points a game. Overbrook High won twenty and lost only two games that season. The team also won the public school title.

Wilt played so well his first year at Overbrook that coaches chose him for Philadelphia's best YMCA team. That team won the national YMCA title and coaches voted Wilt an All-American.

At age sixteen, Wilt stood six feet eleven inches tall. Although tall for the sport, track and field still interested him. At Overbrook, Wilt set records in the 440- and 880-yard running events. Then he broke shot-put and broad jump records. Wilt also ran well in cross-country meets.

Overbrook High didn't lose one basketball game during Wilt's junior year. He scored thirty-seven points per game. As a senior, Wilt was even better, scoring fifty points per game! In one game, he scored ninety points!

In school work, Wilt scored high, too. He earned a B average while taking math, science, speech, English, and French.

Many colleges wanted Wilt to attend their school and play ball for them. He had a tough time choosing one to attend. Almost every weekend

Wilt flew to a different college to see which one he liked best.

Choosing a school was fun for a while, but soon the pressure bothered Wilt. Some coaches even called his home and rang his doorbell when he was sleeping. Some offered Wilt much more than a basketball scholarship. Money and gifts tempted Wilt, but he took neither.

On May 14, 1955, Wilt decided to attend the University of Kansas. Many asked why he was going to a school so far from home. Some people thought

At Kansas Wilt lived in a dormitory that was only for students with athletic scholarships.

Wilt goes above everyone else to score for Kansas.

Wilt was getting illegal money and gifts to go to Kansas.

"All I'm getting is a scholarship," Wilt said, "for tuition, room, and board. I'm also getting $15 a month for laundry and other expenses. I'm not getting any extra money or gifts."

Before he played basketball in Kansas, Wilt had to help solve a racial problem there. Since he was black, some restaurants wouldn't serve him. Instead of fighting, he just sat and waited patiently. Finally, the restaurants decided to serve him and other blacks.

Wilt played his first college basketball game against Northwestern. He scored fifty-two points and grabbed thirty-one rebounds! With Wilt's help that season, Kansas had its best record in twenty years. The team won twenty and lost two, and won the Big Eight title.

Although Wilt played basketball well for Kansas, he had to face more racial problems. During the NCAA finals someone burned a cross in front of his motel room. Then, when Wilt tried to go to a movie, he wasn't allowed in the theater.

When Kansas didn't win the NCAA title, some people blamed Wilt and called him a "loser." Wilt was unhappy because he knew he had played well. He was, however, voted the tournament's best player.

Wilt enjoyed being a disc jockey at Kansas. He

called his show "Flippin' with the Dipper." Wilt played all the hit records of the day and talked with guests. Sometimes he even played his bongo drums on the air.

Bowling, weight lifting, and hand wrestling took up the rest of Wilt's free time. "Wilt's the only man I ever hand wrestled that I couldn't beat," said Bill Neider, an Olympic shot-put star.

The summer after his sophomore year, Wilt spent many hours playing basketball. He played in pickup games all over the East and Midwest. In New York City, Wilt played in schoolyard games against college and pro stars. Many of those stars played better than Wilt. "Those games," Wilt said, "improved my skills more than college games."

During Wilt's junior year, Kansas didn't play well enough to win any basketball titles. That made Wilt unhappy. He didn't even feel like going to school. That year some players tried to knock Wilt down and hurt him. College basketball was no longer fun for Wilt. In the spring, he quit school and left Kansas.

The Harlem Globetrotters basketball team had always thrilled Wilt. After quitting college, he played for the Globetrotters and earned about $65,000 per year. A kind man, Wilt used most of the money to buy his father a new car and his family a new home.

Although Wilt enjoyed many laughs with the

Wilt gives a demonstration of ball control to his new boss, Abe Saperstein, owner of the Globetrotters.

Globetrotters, he wanted to test his skills against the pros in the NBA. In 1959, he signed to play with the Philadelphia Warriors for $100,000 per year.

On October 24, 1959, Wilt played his first pro game. Against the New York Knicks in Madison Square Garden, he scored forty-three points and grabbed eight rebounds!

Wilt quickly found out that pro basketball was a tough sport. He lost eight to twelve pounds during each game. After the games, Wilt drank two or

For his efforts during the 1959-60 season, Wilt was voted rookie of the year and the best player in the NBA.

20

three gallons of milk, orange juice, or pop.

As a pro, Wilt played well until he was hurt. A player jabbed his elbow into Wilt's mouth. Wilt's two front teeth were knocked into the roof of his mouth and he had to have surgery.

In a short time, Wilt recovered and played again. He broke nine records that season! Wilt had the highest scoring record (37.6) and the most rebounds per game (26.9). He was voted rookie of the year as well as the best player. That was the first time a player ever won both awards in the same year.

"WILT QUITS PRO BALL."

The headline shocked the sports world at the end of Wilt's first pro season.

"Why?" fans asked.

"I don't like the way I'm coached," Wilt complained. "I'm not allowed to shoot when I have an open shot. The referees don't call fouls when other players push and shove me. My body aches all over."

Rude fans also made Wilt want to quit playing. When he went for a walk, people pointed at him and laughed at his long legs. Fans expected him to talk to them when he was trying to relax. Wilt couldn't even enjoy meals in restaurants. Fans asked for his autograph while he was eating. Since he couldn't enjoy going out, Wilt spent many hours alone.

Wilt scores two points the easy way!

A shy man, Wilt wanted privacy. "I was never able to go out without being bothered," he said. "The balcony of my New York apartment faced Central Park. I looked down on boys strolling with their girls and envied them. I wondered what it would be like to be an average height. I never liked standing out in a crowd. I wanted to walk down the street and have no one notice me."

Despite his problems with the pros and fans, Wilt still enjoyed the game of basketball. During the summer of 1960, he toured Russia with the Harlem Globetrotters and had fun. In the fall, Wilt changed his mind and decided to play pro ball again.

The 1960-61 season was great for Wilt. He broke all nine records he set in his first season! Then, he set one more record, for the highest field goal percentage (50.5 percent). Wilt was the first NBA player to make more than half his shots!

Free throw shooting started to cause Wilt problems that season. In many games, he missed more free throws than he made. He worked many hours, but it didn't help. "I know the problem is all in my head," Wilt said. "I shoot free throws well in practice." For the rest of his career, Wilt had problems making free throws.

Traveling took much of Wilt's free time between seasons. "The fjords of Norway fascinate me the most," he said. "I speak French well. I under-

It was common for Wilt to stand "head and shoulders" above everyone else.

**Wilt hauls in another rebound in a 1961 game against the Detroit Pistons.**

stand German and Italian, some Spanish and a little Persian. The only way you can really become good at a language is to use it. I've gone many times to different countries and have been able to talk with the people."

Wilt had a speech problem for many years. He worked hard to improve and finally overcame stuttering.

Although Wilt became a good public speaker, he wouldn't talk to students at sports banquets. "I think they're in a fake setting," he said. "All your presence does is give the kids false hopes. How many of them are ever likely to be Wilt Chamberlains?"

Super is the only word to describe Wilt's third season in the pros. He scored one hundred points in one game and averaged fifty points per game! Wilt set ten records that stood for many years. However, he was unhappy because his team didn't win the NBA title.

CHAPTER 4

The next season, the Philadelphia Warriors moved to San Francisco, California. Wilt played well there, leading the league in scoring (44.8 points per game) and rebounding (24.3 per game). Those records weren't enough for Wilt. "The season was a failure," he said. "The team lost many games."

Wilt enjoyed going to movies when he wasn't playing basketball. "My all-time favorites," he said,

This basket on October 30, 1962 put Wilt over the ten thousand point mark during the three years of his playing in the NBA.

"are BRIDGE ON THE RIVER KWAI; BEN HUR; and THE GUNS OF NAVARONE. I must have seen BRIDGE in seven different languages. Movie theaters are one of the places I can go without being bothered. When the lights go out, I go in and slouch down in a seat. Then, I'm just another guy with a box of popcorn."

During the 1963-64 basketball season, Wilt won the scoring title again. He averaged thirty-six points per game. However, scoring wasn't that important to Wilt. He wanted his team to win the title. When they didn't, it bothered him.

The San Francisco Warriors traded Wilt to the Philadelphia 76ers in the 1964-65 season. It was a rough season for Wilt. Several Philadelphia fans booed him. They wanted Wilt to score many points. When he didn't play well, fans called him names. Wilt was the superstar the fans loved to hate.

"The world is made up of Davids," Wilt said, "I am a Goliath, and nobody roots for Goliath."

That season, Wilt weighed about 270 pounds. He was seven feet tall. Wilt was one of basketball's fastest runners and strongest players.

Slower, weaker players tried to stop Wilt by shoving him away from the basket. "The referees don't call fouls on smaller players," Wilt said. "They feel sorry for them." After games Wilt felt worn out. He'd spent too much of his energy dribbling away from small players.

To maintain his energy, Wilt had to eat a lot. One gallon of orange sherbet and orange juice, mixed in a blender, was Wilt's usual breakfast.

Three cheeseburgers, three plates of french fries, three quarts of milk, and three bowls of ice cream was a typical snack for Wilt.

For dinner, Wilt often ate a whole chicken, a plate full of shrimp, cheese, coffee, orange juice, and pastries.

Wilt didn't eat costly meals all the time. "Often," he laughed, "I'm content to dine on hot dogs."

In 1965-66, Wilt had another great season! He led the league in scoring and rebounding. The 76ers had a good season, but lost in the play-offs.

Being a pro basketball player is not easy, even for strong Wilt Chamberlain. "The tough schedule wears me out," he said. "I get tired of the traveling, the plane rides, the airline terminals and hotel rooms."

Suddenly, during the 1966-67 season, Wilt changed his style. Instead of shooting so often, he passed to his teammates. Wilt's new game plan worked well. The Philadelphia 76ers finally won the NBA title! "I feel great!" Wilt told sportswriters.

In the 1967-68 season, Wilt set an important record. He made 702 assists. "I got more happiness out of that record," he said, "than almost any other record. I showed people I could pass the ball to my

Wilt made this free throw in 1966 to score the twenty thousandth point in his NBA career.

Wilt and his Great Danes soak up the sun in front of his house in Bel-Air, California.

32

teammates. The record proved I was more than a giant who could just dunk the ball. It proved I was willing to share the glory of scoring."

Before the 1968-69 season, Wilt was traded to the Los Angeles Lakers. The team and Wilt played well until the Boston Celtics beat them and won the NBA title

# CHAPTER 5

Social problems were still a concern of Wilt's. Instead of just talking, he did something. "I believe the best way I can help blacks," he said, "is by setting a good example. I use my money to open businesses for blacks and give them jobs."

Wilt owned apartment buildings in Los Angeles, New York, Philadelphia, and San Francisco. He also owned music and record companies, race horses, and a travel agency. "I hire black men and women," Wilt said. "But, I make my own deals because I make the best deals for myself."

Dogs always found a special place in Wilt's heart. He spent many happy hours with his own pet dogs. "I have three big, beautiful Great Danes," he said. Their names were Thor, Odin, and Careem. "I really enjoy running, wrestling, and playing with them. I like Great Danes because they're strong. They have so much dignity. I can tell they miss me when I'm gone, and I miss them, too."

A torn tendon in Wilt's right knee hurt him in the 1969-70 season. He had to have knee surgery, which is very serious for athletes. Doctors weren't sure Wilt would ever play again. "That's the kind of challenge I love," Wilt said. "When someone tells me it's impossible, I do it."

This was the most important time in Wilt's life. "I had to will myself to get well," he said, "all the way well. I really wanted to play basketball again. I wanted to play in less than five months!"

For Wilt, the hardest part of getting well was just after surgery. He had to lie flat on his back all the time. "I'd always been an active guy," Wilt said, "and that was tough. I couldn't move, go anywhere, or do anything."

A few weeks later, doctors gave Wilt a tough running and weight lifting program. "Whatever they told me to do," Wilt said, "I doubled it. If they said I should run five miles, I ran ten. If they said I should lift ten pounds with my leg, I lifted twenty."

Every day for an hour, Wilt lifted weights with his leg. He started with twelve pounds and built up to one hundred and fifty pounds. After weight lifting, Wilt rested for a few minutes. Then he walked eight or ten miles through the sand on the beach, fast, without stopping. It took him three or four

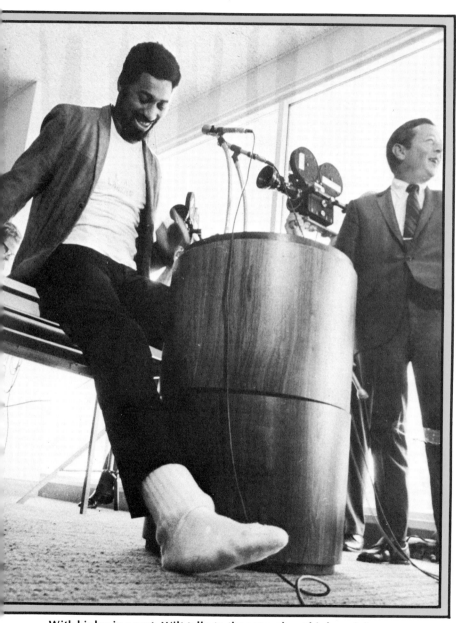

With his leg in a cast, Wilt talks to the press about his knee injury.

Wilt keeps his eye on the ball — a volleyball, this time.

hours to walk that far. Walking helped Wilt get back his wind and strength. It also made his knee and leg strong again.

After his walk, Wilt lifted weights for another hour. Before he went to bed, he again lifted weights for an hour.

Ten hours per day, seven days per week, Wilt worked on strengthening his leg. "Sometimes it was as hopeless," Wilt said, "as it was painful. At first, every time I bent the knee, it felt like someone was running a hot ice pick through the joint. It was just brutal. When the pain lessened a little, I knew I was going to make it."

Volleyball also helped Wilt get better. Playing the game in the sand made both of his legs stronger than ever.

While he recovered, Wilt learned something that changed his life. "I was forced to do some thinking about myself and my life," he said. "I had to take stock of Wilt Chamberlain, the man."

Wilt thought he'd given his best for basketball. Now that would have to be good enough. He was through having to prove himself, again and again. "I'm the best scorer in history," Wilt said. "Why should I have to play better than that?"

Money became less important to Wilt. He used to go out with $5,000 to $10,000 or more stuffed in his pants pockets. After thinking about that, Wilt stopped carrying large sums of money. Most of the

Even Wilt could miss. Here he comes up a bit short on a dunk shot!

time $20 was all he had in his pockets.

Food and clothes didn't excite Wilt as they had before. "I had more fun playing volleyball," he said. "I had the time of my life on the beach in bare feet and a pair of $2.98 shorts. I played volleyball all day, day after day. Maybe I'd spend fifty cents on some lemonade."

"I found out," Wilt said, "just how little I really needed to be happy. I didn't need basketball, fans, or money to be content. Soon, winning NBA titles and flashing $100 bills around didn't mean much to me."

However, Wilt still wanted to play pro ball. He started playing again in March, 1970. When the Lakers didn't win the NBA title, Wilt wasn't upset because he'd done his best.

Music helped Wilt relax after games. He liked country-and-western, blues, jazz, hard rock, and soul music. Beethoven, Schubert, and Wagner also pleased him. Wilt had a sound system in his house with thirty-five to forty speakers.

In 1970-71 Wilt played some of the best basketball of his life. The Lakers, though, failed to make the last round of the play-offs.

**Wilt drives toward the basket in a 1971 game against the New York Knicks.**

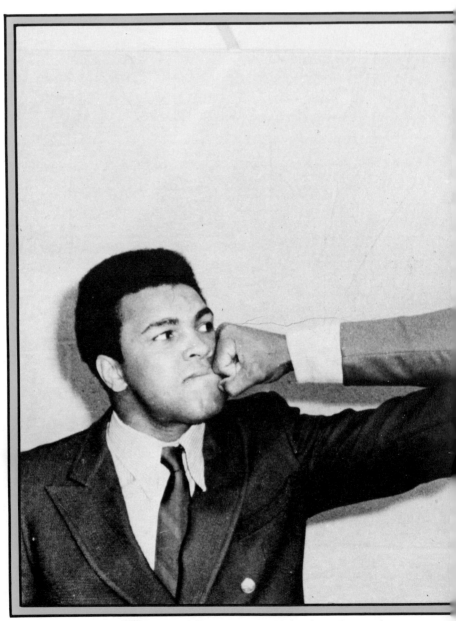

In a playful mood in 1971, Wilt and former Heavyweight Champion, Muhammad Ali, checked out each other's reach.

# CHAPTER 6

The team didn't give up. They practiced more, and it paid off in 1971-72. The Lakers became one of the best basketball teams ever. With Wilt's help, they won thirty-three games in a row. They broke every record in the book that season and had the most wins, both at home and on the road. The Lakers' season record was sixty-nine wins and just thirteen losses.

A broken hand didn't stop Wilt in the play-offs. He played with a splint, and helped the Lakers beat the New York Knicks to win the NBA title. Sportswriters voted Wilt the best player of the series.

In the 1972-73 season, Wilt played well. For the tenth time, he led the league in field goal percentage. His field goal record (73%) set an all-time mark!

Pain slowed Wilt down in the NBA title game. He played with one swollen eye, two fingers taped together, and a hamstring pull. His heel was so sore he could hardly walk on it. The Lakers lost the NBA title to the New York Knicks.

After that season, Wilt retired from playing pro basketball. "I've played enough," he said, "and the

Wilt stuffs in two points against the Milwaukee Bucks in a 1972 game.

fun is gone."

Coaching also excited Wilt. In the 1973-74 season, he led the San Diego Conquistadors in the American Basketball Association (ABA). The Q's tied for last, with a 37-47 mark. Wilt felt so bad he quit coaching basketball.

In 1974-75, Wilt had fun leading a women's volleyball team. "I called them," Wilt said, "the Little Dippers."

A super athlete, Wilt was the first to say he was not a super human. "I'm short on patience," he said. "I open my mouth too quickly and speak too bluntly."

Working hard, Wilt changed his life. He became more casual and relaxed. However, he knew he couldn't please everyone. "I'm honest, so I must speak up when things upset me," he said. "I am sorry when I hurt people. People's feelings mean a lot to me. I have more friends than enemies, and will do anything for them."

Young people were always very important to Wilt. "I'm probably the only superstar," he said, "who still plays in schoolyard pick up games. I'll play with a bunch of kids just for the fun of the game."

Living a happy life was more important to Wilt than playing basketball. "I have made a lot of my life," he said. "I've done a lot and if I lost all tomorrow, I couldn't complain."

Wilt announces to the press that he was going to join the Conquistadors of the ABA as a player-coach.

Wilt takes a relaxing stroll along the beach — something he now has the time to do quite often.

At the end of his career, Wilt told sportswriters, "Basketball has been good to me. I love the game, and I always will."

Wilt Chamberlain was great for basketball. Thousands of fans enjoyed watching him play. Fans can't ask for more from a sports legend than Wilt Chamberlain gave.

**AFTERWORD:**

Wilt Chamberlain is currently living in Los Angeles, California. He owns and manages several businesses. One job that takes much of his time is managing apartment buildings.

When Wilt has free time, he enjoys playing volleyball and walking on the beach along the Pacific Ocean.

# IF YOU ENJOYED THIS STORY, THERE ARE MORE LEGENDS TO READ ABOUT: